The Horror of the Heights

Anthony Masters

Illustrated by Peter Dennis

A & C Black • London

GRAFFIX

First paperback edition 2000
First published 2000 in hardback by
A & C Black (Publishers) Ltd
35 Bedford Row, London WC1R 4JH

ISBN 0-7136-5385-X

A CIP catalogue for this book is available from
the British Library.

Printed and bound in Spain by G. Z. Printek, Bilbao.

Chapter One

Dean Lambert gazed up at the Horror of the Heights, as he had nicknamed the high diving board at Wave Crest Leisure Centre.

Now he was determined to conquer his fear.

Dean's dad was the manager of the leisure centre. His older brother Tim was a champion diver. The two of them watched anxiously as Dean started to climb the ladder to the top board.

Not daring to look down, Dean slowly climbed on, the fear of failing just a shade worse than the fear of jumping.

Dean stood for a long time on the top rung of the ladder, not able to force himself out on to the board. There were beads of sweat on his forehead and his heart was pounding so hard it hurt.

He glanced down, only to see Dad [...]
up at him, willing him on. They [...]
wanted him to succeed.

You can do it, De[...]

But Dean knew he couldn't.
He could never stand on that swaying top board,
staring down at the dark blue water below.
It would be impossible.

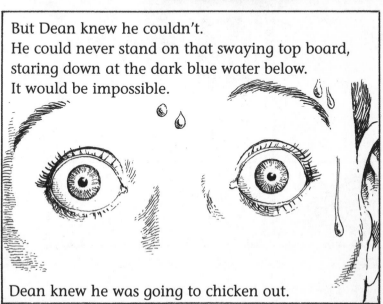

Dean knew he was going to chicken out.

ashamed, he slowly began to climb down.
he reached the side of the pool, his father,
Lambert, was already waiting for him.

ke spoke quietly.

Pity.
Bad luck, son.

Then he walked hurriedly away.

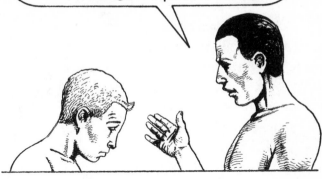

Dean was miserable.

Tim tried to reassure his brother.

No way.
It's just that the car crash is still getting to him. He can't forgive himself for killing the other driver, even though the police have told him it wasn't his fault.

Tim climbed up the long ladder to the board.
He made it look so easy. Dean watched enviously.
In a few days Tim was going to take part in an important regional high diving competition, hosted by Wave Crest.

Tim stood on the top board and waved down at Dean. He then took a run, prepared to dive.

Suddenly the board collapsed, making him fall awkwardly down into the pool, catching his ankle on the springboard below.

Without thinking, Dean leapt after him into the diving pool - even though he hated being out of his depth. He was a fast swimmer though, and he soon reached Tim, who was floating on his back, spluttering.

Tim was grinning but also wincing with pain.

12

Tim hauled himself up on to the side of the pool and Dean followed.

Wait a minute. You were out of your depth back there.

So?

Tim put his arm round Dean's shoulders.

You did that for me, didn't you?

What if I did?

Luke Lambert inspected the board.

A bolt's worked loose. I'm going to ring Ken.

He went off to find Ken Drake, the centre's maintenance engineer as well as the swimming coach.

That's weird, isn't it? Ken inspects all the equipment every day. How could he have missed that?

Maybe the bolt suddenly worked loose.

Tim looked worried.

It doesn't happen like that.

Chapter Two

Next day, Ken Drake and Luke Lambert were putting some of the young divers through their paces, including Tim and Ben Robinson, his closest rival.

Dean decided to watch, still anxious about his brother's ankle. But the bruising didn't seem to bother Tim as he took his turn, diving from the top board, which Ken had made safe again.

Ken was encouraging. Dad wasn't.
He was yelling at Tim.

Come on, Tim!
What are you doing?
That's no good!
You can't afford to be off-form.
The competition's in a couple of days.

Dean noticed that Ben was watching Tim closely, no doubt enjoying hearing him criticised. Dean had never liked Ben. He had a huge ego and was a lousy loser.

At the end of the session, Dean was even more worried as he overheard a row between Dad and Ken Drake. They were shouting at each other so loudly it would have been impossible not to hear them.

You're pushing Tim too hard. You'll break him. He'll lose all his confidence.

Rubbish! He's not working hard enough.

Who's the coach round here? You or me?

You're too soft.

Ken walked away into the changing rooms, leaving the few divers still practising looking awkward and embarrassed. One of them was Tim.

Chapter Three

There was a pool-side disco that evening to celebrate the opening of Raging Waters, the new flumes at the leisure centre. Tim and Dean went along with Maggie and Dawn, two of the Wave Crest lifesavers.

Swimmers entered the twisting tubes at the top, plunging through the labyrinth on a stream of water and tumbling into a plunge pool at the bottom. There were three flumes, each more scary than the last.

The flumes were proving to be a very popular new attraction, and there was a long queue of men, women and older children waiting to try it out.

Dean and Maggie were dancing together when they heard a scream and cries of pain coming from the plunge pool.

They raced over to where a boy was clambering out with a badly cut arm. His father was already there and very angry indeed. Luke Lambert was quickly on the scene, looking horrified.

Luke kept apologising to the father while an attendant dried the boy's arm and applied first aid.

Later that night the investigation began as the staff stripped away the plastic sides of the Twister, the flume that had given all the trouble.
Luke Lambert was angry.

23

Afterwards Dean and Maggie walked home through the dark winter streets. Dean liked Maggie a lot. She was funny and attractive, and seemed to like him too. She was the first girl who hadn't treated him as a kid.

At the moment Dean had other things on his mind. He was not only worried about Wave Crest, but Tim too. Suppose another piece of equipment collapsed on him? He could be very badly hurt.

Then there was Dad to consider. He'd been so quiet and withdrawn since the crash, but also mean-spirited and bad tempered. These incidents at Wave Crest weren't going to bring back the old Dad, who was kind and generous and good to be with.

Maggie was suspicious.

What for?

I want to check out and see if someone's trying to sabotage Wave Crest and I could use some support.

Maggie shivered.

You mean someone might be getting in after hours and deliberately doing damage?

Dean could see how scared she was. He didn't feel that good himself.

Maggie snapped at him.

Chapter Four

The leisure centre was eerie without its customers. All Dean and Maggie could hear from their hiding place in the storeroom the following evening was the clanking of the air-conditioning system and the gurgling of water in the pools.

Maggie grabbed Dean's shoulder.

I think I can hear someone moving.

But when they arrived in the gloom of the diving pool, lit only by a couple of security lights, neither Maggie nor Dean could see anything to arouse their suspicions.

Who's got keys besides your dad?

Only Ken Drake.

They don't hit it off well, do they?

Dean felt defensive about his father.

What do you mean?

Didn't they have a row recently?
One of many?

It's not that bad.

Isn't it?

Chapter Five

The next day, Luke Lambert was furious when he heard on the grapevine what Dean and Maggie had done.

You two ought to be thoroughly ashamed of yourselves.

Maggie looked down at the floor. Dean spoke anxiously.

We wanted to catch whoever was responsible for the sabotage. It was my idea –

I'm sure it was. Only you could be stupid enough to try and pull off a stunt like that.

That evening a large audience sat around the pool as the young divers nervously awaited the beginning of the competition. Dean and Maggie, who was off-duty, had got good seats just beside the high diving board. On the lower section of the opposite tier were Luke Lambert and Ken Drake, near the line of judges. All the divers' supporters were there.

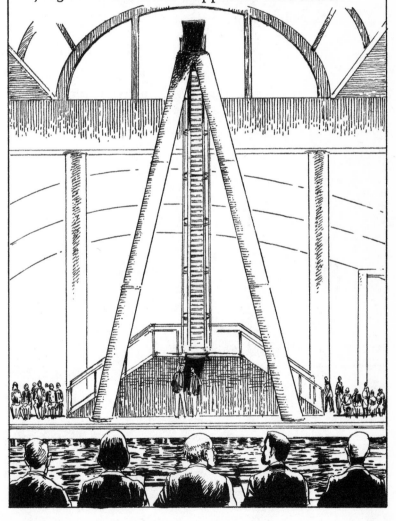

Dean was gazing up at the equipment, wondering if it could have been sabotaged again, despite the fact that Dad had told him everything had been checked over just before the audience were seated.

Could anyone have had a go at it since then?

Then Dean's thoughts switched to the saboteur and he glanced around the spectators.

Maggie shrugged.

36

Dawn passed by. Dean leant out and whispered to her.

Has anyone been near the diving boards since they were last checked?

No one.

Unless you count Ken Drake, of course. I did see him making a few adjustments to the high diving board.

Dean's tension increased so much he could hardly sit still. Looking up at the clock on the wall of the pool he saw the diving competition was due to start in two minutes time.

Dean was out of his mind with anxiety. The contestants were lining up now and he could see his brother was going to be the first to dive.

He could hardly bear to watch.

Dean stood up as a fanfare of canned music announced the beginning of the competition.
What are you going to do?
I'm going to put a stop to all this.

Ken Drake rose to his feet and adjusted the microphone.

Ladies and gentlemen. Welcome to the Southern Regional High Diving Competition at the Wave Crest Leisure Centre.

My name's Ken Drake and I'm going to be your commentator this afternoon. Our first competitor for the High Dive is Tim Lambert. Tim has a -

But Dean was no longer listening. He was edging along the row of seats and running on to the side of the pool, hurrying towards his brother.

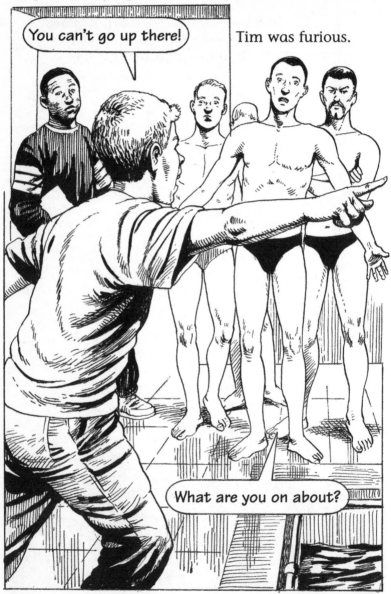

Tim was furious.

45

The audience was alarmed now. Some people were rising to their feet and asking questions that no one could answer. The muttering grew to an agitated roar.

The board could have been sabotaged - in the last half hour.

Dean was desperate enough to be almost convincing, and his father paused.

I'll *go and see.*

Luke Lambert looked grim as he began to head for the ladder. Dean noticed that Ken Drake was gazing up in alarm. The spectators were quiet now as his father carefully inspected the top board. Then his shoulders sagged and Dean knew with a sickening lurch inside that he'd been right – there was something wrong.

Luke quickly descended the ladder.

A bolt's been removed. Again.

Ken came up, looking horrified.

Another one?
I don't believe this.

Luke Lambert choked with emotion.

Tim turned to Dean in bewilderment.

How did you know?

I didn't. I had this - hunch.

He walked back to Maggie.

Who left the diving pool last? Ken or Dawn? Or was Ben lurking about somewhere?

He briefly glanced down the side of the pool at Ben, who was looking devastated. Maggie paused uneasily.

Come on. You must remember.

I think it was Dawn who left last.

Chapter Six

Dawn had moved round to the side of the pool and was leaning against the wall. Without hesitating any longer, Dean began to run towards her, so wild with fury that he felt almost out of control. He could kill her. She could have killed his brother.

Dawn gazed at him in amazement, but when she saw the murderous look in Dean's eyes she cringed back in fear.

Dawn looked at him in horror.

Watched by the incredulous spectators, she began
to run along the side of the pool, hotly
pursued by Dean.

Maggie was behind him now as Dean chased Dawn
out of the diving area and into the main complex
where the evening swimming session was almost
over. The flumes were closing and most people were
making for the showers.

Dawn was heading for the flumes, but as she ran up the slope towards the top of RAGING WATERS, she tripped and fell.

Although she got back on her feet quickly, Dean knew that the gap between them had narrowed.

A boy of about his own age yelled at him.

Stop chasing that girl! She's a friend of -

Dean gave him a hard shove in the chest that sent him flying back.

Get out of my way!

Dean and Maggie were only a metre behind Dawn now and he felt a wild surge of triumph as he realised she couldn't escape. Then one of the attendants called to Dawn.

What's up? Fancy a trip down the Twister?

As she plunged in head-first, the attendant gasped.

One moment Dawn was there. The next moment she wasn't, and Dean gave an angry cry of rage. He turned back to Maggie.

Grab her when she comes out into the plunge pool.

Maggie doubled back, bumped into someone and ran on, leaving him sprawling.

What's going on? This a charity stunt or something? Mr Lambert should have told –

But Dean wasn't listening. Instead, clad in tee-shirt, jeans and trainers, he followed Dawn down the swirling waters of the Twister.

Fully dressed, the ride down the Twister was incredibly uncomfortable as Dean was whipped from one side to another, the flume carrying him through all kinds of blind corners and sudden drops. Soaked and gasping, he was finally flung down into the plunge pool.

When Dean surfaced he could see Dawn and Maggie struggling together in the shallows. Dawn was shouting.

What's the matter with you two? I haven't done anything. I haven't done anything at all.

She was crying now and no longer attempting to wrench herself out of Maggie's grip.

As Dean staggered towards them in his wringing wet clothes, weighed down by his trainers, a feeble cheer went up from the spectators.

Luke Lambert was staring at the bedraggled threesome, still wading in the plunge pool while the crowd grew larger around them.

Well?
What can you prove, Maggie?

She stood there silently, staring at Dean, and suddenly he knew. There was something in that look. Something that told him everything. But why?

Come on... I'm waiting.

I did it.

Did what?

You killed my father. That's why.

Shivering, draped in towels, Dean, Maggie and Dawn sat in Luke Lambert's office, drinking tea they didn't want.

Luke was deeply shocked.

You hated me that much?

My father was everything to me.

It wasn't Dad's fault.

I just wanted to destroy him. I couldn't bear him to get away with it. So I came to work here at Wave Crest and - learnt the ropes.

You learnt to sabotage equipment.

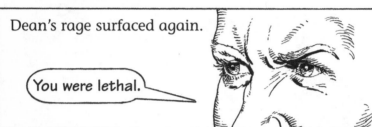

Dean's rage surfaced again.

You were lethal.

Maggie looked away.

You did some terrible things, Maggie. And Dean's right - you could have killed someone. Like my son. Like anyone.

Chapter Seven

Dean and Tim walked towards the high diving board. The pool was closed and no one was around – not even Dad.

As Dean began to climb the ladder, hands and knees shaking, he tried to distract himself by thinking about what Dad had done for Maggie. He still couldn't believe his father had let her off, despite what she had done and how much she had hated him.

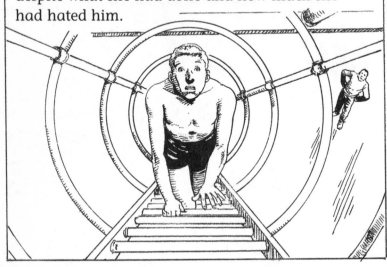

Tim broke into his thoughts.

Go for it!
It's going to be okay!

As Dean climbed on, his breath coming in little gasps and sweat pouring down his face, his father's words still rang in his ears.

What I'm going to do, Maggie, is ring your mum and suggest we three all have a chat. You need some help.

Dean knew he hadn't heard his father talk like this for ages. In fact, ever since Maggie had made her confession, Dad seemed to have become his old self again, despite everything.

Dean was shaking now as he reached the Horror of the Heights. When he got to the top rung of the ladder, he froze. This was where he had failed before.

Dean closed his eyes.

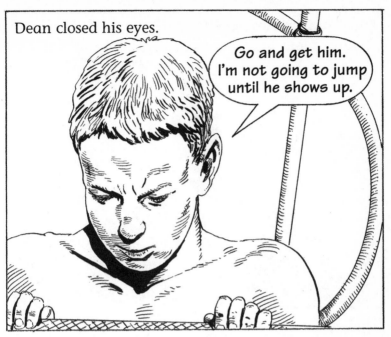

Go and get him.
I'm not going to jump
until he shows up.

Tim ran out – and returned almost immediately
with their father. Dean realised he must have been
waiting somewhere nearby.

Why didn't you come to watch?

Luke Lambert strolled towards him.

I'm here now. Go for it.

Dad made it sound as if the jump would be easy.

Slowly Dean pulled himself over the last rung. He reached the board and crouched on his hands and knees. For a few moments he stayed where he was, arms and legs trembling. He felt like jelly.

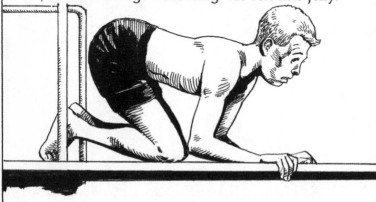

Dean knew he'd never stand on jelly legs.

The dark blue water below looked cruel and distant. Suppose he jumped wide? Would he fall on to the side of the pool and break his arms and legs? Might he break his neck and die a terrible death or be crippled for life?

Dean looked down at his father who was now casually leaning against the wall. Only Tim seemed agitated as he gazed up.

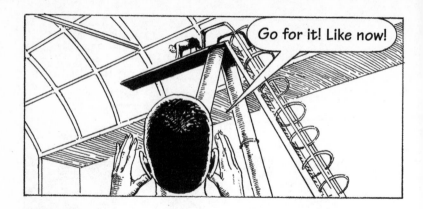

Go for it! Like now!

Dean tried to get to his feet, but his jelly arms and legs wouldn't let him. He stayed crouching, smelling the chlorine, listening to the water in the pool sloshing slightly against the sides. It was waiting for him.

Dean wiped away the sweat from his eyes and struggled to his feet.

Then his father's kind words to Maggie filtered his fear, calmly, reassuringly. 'I told you – you need some help. Let's sort it out with your mother. Try not to hate me any more.'

'I don't,' Maggie had sobbed. 'I really don't.'

Dean staggered to the edge of the board. There seemed to be a roaring in his ears and for a moment he almost overbalanced.

Then he slowly lifted his arms.
The board was swaying. So was he.

Dean jumped.

He landed in the pool with the most enormous
splash and the relief soared in him so much that
he almost felt light-headed.

Dad and Tim were leaping about, clapping and cheering, and suddenly Dean had never felt so happy in his life.

Then, to his amazement, he realised he was swimming comfortably in deep water. Dean was out of his depth but he couldn't care less.

He swam over to his father and brother and they each grabbed an arm and triumphantly pulled him out of the pool, hugging him and not even thinking about getting their clothes damp.

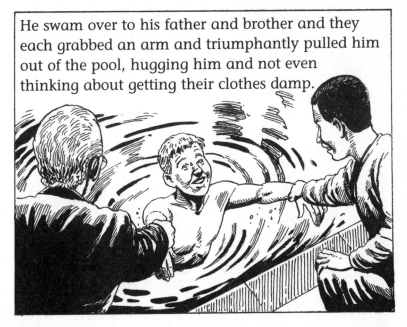

Tim thumped him on the back so hard it hurt.

You've done it!

Dad was as delighted as Tim.

Brilliant! Absolutely brilliant. Now go back and do it again.

I don't mind if I do.

Dean ran towards the ladder and began to clamber up to the Horror of the Heights. But it wasn't horrifying any more.

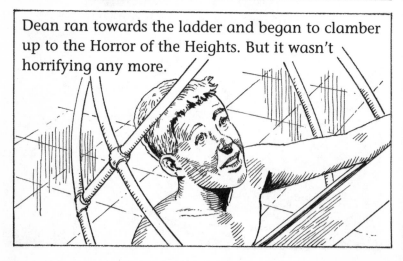